ALWAYS STICK UP FOR THE UNDERBIRD

BONG!

Peanuts Parade Paperbacks

ALWAYS STICK UP FOR THE UNDERBIRD

Cartoons from *Good Grief, More Peanuts!* and *Good Ol' Charlie Brown*

by Charles M. Schulz

Holt, Rinehart and Winston / New York

Published simultaneously in Canada by Holt, Rinehart
and Winston of Canada, Limited.

First published in this form in 1977.

Library of Congress Catalog Card Number: 76-43500
ISBN: 0-03-020671-5

Printed in the United States of America

10 9 8 7 6 5 4 3 2

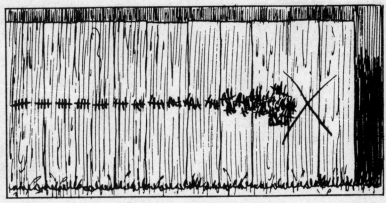

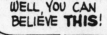
 YOU CAN'T BELIEVE EVERYTHING YOU HEAR, YOU KNOW..

 WELL, YOU CAN BELIEVE **THIS**!

 YOU **KNOW** I'M RIGHT, SCHROEDER..

 IF YOU HAD ANY SENSE AT ALL, YOU'D ADMIT IT..

 OH, YEAH?

 YOU JUST SAY THAT BECAUSE YOU'RE STUPID, CHARLIE BROWN!

 **STUPID?** LISTEN TO WHO'S TALKING!

 YOU AND THAT **PIANO** OF YOURS ARE THE **STUPID** ONES!

 PLINK PLINK PLINK!! ALL DAY LONG... **GOOD GRIEF!**

 WELL, HOW ABOUT YOU AND THAT SILLY OL' COONSKIN CAP?!

 AND HOW ABOUT THAT STUPID SHIRT WITH THAT STUPID STRIPE?!

 WELL, AT LEAST, SCHROEDER, I DON'T HAVE YELLOW HAIR!

 NO, BUT YOU SURE HAVE A ROUND HEAD!

 WHAT IN THE WORLD IS GOING ON HERE?

 WE'RE ARGUING OVER WHO WAS THE BETTER...BEETHOVEN OR DAVY CROCKETT!

 **WHO'S** GOT A ROUND HEAD? **YOU** HAVE!

SCHULZ

KLUNK!

SCHULZ

WELL? WHAT DO YOU THINK? SHALL WE DO SOMETHING ELSE FOR AWHILE?

WE MIGHT AS WELL...LET'S GO OVER TO MY HOUSE FOR SOME LEMONADE..

WHEW!

WHEN? WHEN? WHEN? WHEN? WHEN? WHEN? WHEN?

WHEN WILL I EVER LEARN?!

SCHULZ

SCHULZ

SCHULZ

WHAT IN THE WORLD IS GOING ON OVER THERE?

?

?

HEY! IS THERE ROOM FOR ONE MORE?

SURE.. COME ON IN!

THE HOUSE ITSELF ISN'T SO BIG, BUT YOU OUGHT TO SEE THE RECREATION ROOM!

SCHULZ

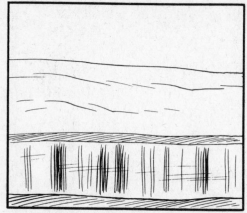

GOOD GRIEF! I THINK I FROZE MY STOMACH!

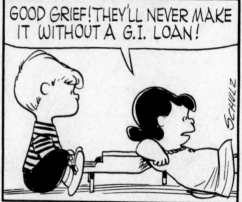

BOY, IF THAT DOESN'T TAKE THE CAKE!

WHAT'S THE MATTER, LUCY?

THAT GIRL IN THE NEXT BLOCK..

SHE GOT MAD JUST BECAUSE I HIT HER BROTHER...

I WOULDN'T GET MAD IF SHE HIT MY BROTHER!

STOP IT! STOP IT THIS INSTANT! WITH ALL THE TROUBLE THERE IS IN THIS WORLD, YOU HAVE NO RIGHT TO BE SO HAPPY!!

SHE'S RIGHT...I'VE GOT TO START ACTING MORE SENSIBLE...

...TOMORROW!

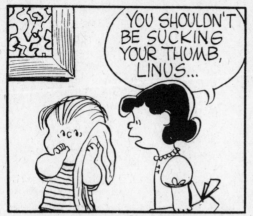

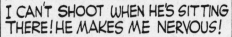

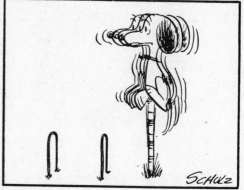

WELL?! WHO'S GOING TO OPEN THE DOOR?!

YOU THINK YOU'RE SMART JUST BECAUSE YOU'RE OLDER THAN I AM!

YOU JUST **HAPPENED** TO BE BORN FIRST THAT'S ALL !!! YOU WERE JUST **LUCKY**!!

I DIDN'T **ASK** TO BE BORN SECOND!

I DIDN'T EVEN GET A CHANCE TO FILL OUT AN APPLICATION!

STOMP

STOMP STOMP STOMP

STOMP STOMP STOMP

THIS OL' WORLD IS IN PRETTY GOOD SHAPE!

THERE'S ONE LITTLE FRAYED SPOT HERE.. ONE LITTLE PLACE...

RIGHT ALONG THE EDGE HERE.. I HAVE TO FIND... RIGHT ALONG HERE..I HAVE TO...RIGHT ABOUT...

AH!

SIGH..

SCHULZ

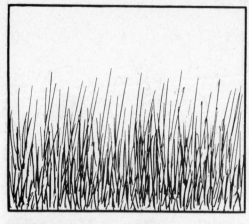

AHCHOO!

CHARLIE BROWN, WOULD YOU LIKE TO COME TO A PARTY SOMETIME NEXT WEEK?

WHY, YES, I'D LIKE THAT VERY MUCH..

I THOUGHT YOU WOULD...BUT I DOUBT IF I'LL INVITE YOU ANYWAY..

THE ONLY TROUBLE WITH LIVING IN THESE NEW HOUSING DEVELOPMENTS IS THERE ARE NO TREES TO HIT YOUR HEAD AGAINST!

SCHULZ

GEE! IT DIDN'T EVEN BREAK..

NOW, YOU KNOW WHAT YOU'RE GOING TO DO TOMORROW NIGHT, DON'T YOU?

SURE.. I JUST GO UP TO THESE DIFFERENT HOUSES, RING THEIR DOORBELLS AND THEN SHOUT, **"TRICKS OR TREATS!"**

SAY, BY THE WAY... THERE'S NO LAW AGAINST THAT, IS THERE?

OF COURSE NOT..

I WOULDN'T WANT TO DO ANYTHING THAT MIGHT AROUSE THE F.B.I.!

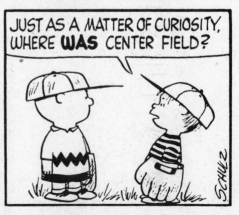